THE GOLDEN BOOK OF WORDS

Other Books by Bernadette Mayer

Story
Moving
Ceremony Latin (1964)
Studying Hunger
Memory
Poetry
Eruditio ex Memoria
Midwinter Day
Utopia
Mutual Aid
Sonnets
The Formal Field of Kissing
A Bernadette Mayer Reader
The Desires of Mothers to Please Others in Letters
Another Smashed Pinecone
Proper Name & Other Stories
Two Haloed Mourners
Indigo Bunting
Scarlet Tanager
What's Your Idea of a Good Time? (with Bill Berkson)
Poetry State Forest
Ethics of Sleep
Studying Hunger Journals
The Helens of Troy, NY
At Maureen's (with Greg Masters)
Uncle Andrew's Pile of Pads
Eating the Colors of a Lineup of Words
Works and Days
Piece of Cake (with Lewis Warsh)
Subatomic Moss (with Philip Good)
The Basketball Article Comic Book (with Anne Waldman, illustrated by Jason Novak)
Milkweed Smithereens

THE GOLDEN BOOK OF WORDS

Bernadette Mayer

A New Directions Paperbook

Certain of the poems in this book have been published in *Zzzzz, Sun & Moon, United Artists, Partisan Review, New World Journal, Bezoar, Shell* and *This*

Original cover design by Joe Brainard used by permission of the Estate of Joe Brainard

Originally published by Angel Hair Books in 1978 in an edition of 750 copies
Published as New Directions Paperbook 1634 in 2025
Manufactured in the United States of America

Library of Congress Cataloging-in-Publication Data has been applied for

10 9 8 7 6 5 4 3 2 1

New Directions Books are published for James Laughlin
by New Directions Publishing Corporation
80 Eighth Avenue, New York 10011

THE GOLDEN BOOK OF
WORDS
BY
BERNADETTE
MAYER

Overleaf: drawing for original cover by Joe Brainard

THE GOLDEN BOOK OF WORDS

for Lewis,

THE GOLDEN BOOK OF WORDS

Why is my verse so barren of new pride,
So far from variation or quick change?
Why with the time do I not glance and hide
The moving scene from memory's compounds strange?
Why write I still all one, ever the same,
Now past the hunger of studying psychology
Yet every word doth almost tell my name
And I delight in slow chronology
These poems transgress the seasons of two years
O, know, sweet love, I always write of you
Each winter's work burgeoning among spring's fears
So all my best is dressing old words new
And you and love are still my argument
Intact as memory when I watch to see
Spending always what is already spent
If traded to poetry night is day's family:

  For as the sun is daily new and old
  Quick change past Shakespeare's steepy memory
  So is my love still telling what is told,
  Time's thievish word to last eternity.

THE END OF HUMAN REIGN ON BASHAN HILL

They come down on their snowmobiles for the last time,
come down to meet the car.
They're shouting, "Hoo Hey! The snow! Give them the snow!
Let them eat snow! Hey! The snow!"
Looking like wild men & women, two wild children & a
grandmother too, they're taking turns riding the
snowmobile, they're getting out.
Hoo! Hey! The snow! freaking out.
Everybody in town watches, standing in groups by the
"Road Closed" sign.
Shouting back, "Take it easy! The snow!"
On Bashan Hill they'd lived in a cloud, watched. They'd had
plenty of split peas, corn, Irish soda bread, fruitcake,
chocolate, pemmican. But the main thing was—NO PLOW!
Day before at the Corners Grocery, news got around. "They're
coming down from Bashan Hill—never to return!"
The snow!
Hey, the snow, you forget. They're coming to get a beer.
Have another beer, smoke, jerk off & be thankful.
They're moving to a place above the store, where they can be
watched. The snowman'll come & watch them, the pie man'll
come & watch them, the UPS man'll come & watch them, the
oil man, the gas man'll watch them, the plow man'll watch
them, the workers on the town roads.
Sink their shovels deep into the winter's accumulation right
before their very eyes, eyes turned blue in the
Arctic night.
The brown-eyed family from Bashan Hill in town for a
postage stamp.
The black-eyed family of deer, the open-eyed rabbits, the
circle-eyed raccoons, the white-eyed bear.
Where do the green frogs winter that look so old?
We watched so carefully our eyes became vacant, our minds
stirred from laughter all the memories of a chant.
Hoo! Hey! The snow!
They've come down the hill we watch in a cloud, night of the
full moon, icy crowd on the road watching them.
Have a piece of chocolate!
Open your eyes!

THE OLYMPICS

I watch the skaters & want to weep for joy
Did you ever wait so long in a season before
For winter to change? The ice only melts & freezes again.
We get in the car & drive to the store, I drink my first beer
        of the day, baby sleeps & I feel great looking out the
        window memorizing these 4.4 miles of landscape going
        slowly by
I want to smoke a cigarette but I dont
The way back with the sun in our eyes, this is my favorite
        part of the day
That & getting into bed at night, trusting, even if there's a
        heavy wind blowing, that the power lines wont go down
        until morning if our bodies are touching
I've learned how to go back to sleep after you get up & sleep
        through your walk down the road to get the mail
This is my most fearful part of the day, unless it's snowing,
        for what if you didnt come back, how would I go & find you
I wont go into that.
The mice or flying squirrels store our almonds all over the
        house, you drop your clothes in a heap & by morning
        they've become a nest, the center of a roll of paper is
        a good storage space
We've seen very few animals this year.
Sometimes I write this way to please you or, forgive me,
        it becomes me to become you as I dream that even plants
        & spoons become a family
We let ourselves get dirty, we bathe all the time, we never
        bathe, a hot bath in winter's a great luxury, naked when
        it's 22 below, daring it to try & come inside
I forget that I was thinking of Bunny Lang
What if a visitor, a stranger came, slammed his car door
        & asked for shelter from the storm
But you say it's still above freezing & will remain so
The sheets are hanging outside, I've had a heavy meal, nothing
        is condensed, you hear an animal, I'd like a drink, we
        could live on pears or find the squirrels' stored nuts,

shake the gourds until they rattle, I dont hear, what
do you hear
My hands have changed, I like to eat pears & even vegetables,
I dream I am the husband of a wife & so I appear changed,
I find our backs are curving way over our tasks
You dont approve of certain things I do, but very few, one of
them might be
I am dressed like an american flag on valentine's day, it's
all by chance, I'd put my saluting spring scarf on & only
noticed my socks were red white & blue, I'd wished for a
red campari & soda, with vodka an americano, the car is
red, my scarlet union suit, my blue dungarees, your
mother's red shoes
I forget I was thinking of the temperature & the sheets
hanging out but there's also our new red blanket & this
poem written in red permanent red ink for tomorrow,
valentine's day
I wanted to get you a basketball & I will
Did you ever wait so long before in a season
If you kiss me it will be spring & not mid-winter suppers
Held like the great Antarctic parties when the darkness there
is half over & the sun will begin to be higher in the sky
or in the sky at all
The same as it will be here where sun rises in our room & sets
in yours
But the best is the clouds behind the barn where the
basketball hoop will go
So winter goes away on valentine's day, we store up squirrels,
singing basketball, we weep olympics, sneer at storms,
flying sheets, the thaw flies into the river bottom,
storing bottles & bright red cans, like detectives,
you need boots we add weight to our bodies in the house,
drive on the ice, there's a crack goes through into
eternity, little below, ever wait so long in a season
before, athletic love in the seasons, we have all the time
in the seasons, protected by all the red love things

LOOKIN LIKE AREAS OF KANSAS

"We had our first cucumber
yesterday"
Nathaniel Hawthorne

New England is awful
The winter's five months long
The sun may come out today but that doesnt mean anything
There are Yankees
Men & women who cant talk
They wear dark colors & trudge around, all in browns & greys,
 looking up at the sky & pretending to predict all the
 big storms
Or else they nod wisely
Yup, a northeaster
The sky turns yellow all the time
The river's grey
Everything's black or white
Everybody eats beans
Everything freezes
Everybody lives in an old paper house
People chop wood all the time
They slide around on these slippery icy roads
All the trees look dead
They make long shadows on the snow
There's only daylight for about four hours
People sit home & drink boilermakers
At night all the telephones go out & the power lines blow down
Every weekend there's a storm so nobody can come to see you
The fireplaces are very drafty
The mountains look black
There are no books at the store
Religion's a big thing
Everybody has a history
Sex is drudgery for people in New England
It's 12° & they use Trojans or Tahitis
Some people have to have a generator

The windows are very small
You have to go out & get cold
All of a sudden the blue sky blows away
Everything's buried under five feet of snow
It doesnt go away until April or May
Everything's either apples or some kind of squash
The houses are all drafty boxes & you cant open the windows
People tell stories about each other
People have to come & plow the snow off to the side of
    your road
Then people shovel pathways to different cars
They have town meetings about the new sewer systems
The ideas of people in general are not raised higher than the
    roofs of their houses
Even the water freezes in the tap

I COULD EAT A HORSE

Took a long walk looking at
The branches bloomed by mistake in early February
Leathery brown leaves now in a field of lobelia
That's a herb that will make you cough, if you want
An expectorant, if you drink a brew of it
A daily extant flower here in the hills behind-the-times
Jack-in-the-pulpits of this more freezing hill of ours
Where spring is late in every way though it came early
No lilacs yet though I've been writing about it since
February
Early February, this is the heaviest wettest day of the
year, May 17
Green worms crawling on the leaves of the phlox
I could eat a horse

WHAT BABIES REALLY DO

Light like the life I'm in
Who said that did you say that did I
Eating doesnt go with prose
or poetry, spaghetti maybe

Out a window cool spring gray day
with only tips of trees in buds
The ground's not wet yet
Something leaps & bounds

Mothers always too specific
Ounces of pounds, silver on silver
I wouldnt actually eat a clam with a spoon
It's too rubbery

Often when I'm happy a fear comes over me –
not fear that the joy will end, but fear that circumstances
beyond my control and unexpected will arise to prevent me
from ever feeling joy again.

We'll get dresses from Boston
like the elation of a sealed fruit
pure banana with the elation
of the afternoon in its skin

Rheingold kasha scotch kooler
I let endless thoughts go by in between
like the rice that looks like a belly
I dont have my own voice

So I quickly end the pleasure
of the first gray day that was truly
brown in the air, many trees
have snapped in half this winter

One big maple threatens the house
with its leaking bark, a crack
right down the side of an arm of it
We agree it'll fall but in what direction

Rice beads rutted road too many things
in my ideas, I like the New Yorker
where the poems have no ideas
I like the gray sappy maples losing their branches over me

The brown road's ok, smell of bananas
Birds are good, you live inside them
We found your slip you should see my view
You forgot to remind me not to have another beer

It's an endless afternoon, it refuses to rain
I fill up my mouth with Dashiell-Hammett-type smoke
It refuses to be consistent
As there are ingredients all over

& more branches, chair legs
& more flour, I sit with the food
Tuna tempter kasha varnishkas
A hundred and one fillets

Not just brown bread
but brown bread with raisins
You order more than five lbs of oranges
I carry a crate in the back of my jeep or keep

Sunflower kernels to replace the sight of one
Life like it is
The gray branches wont move
unless wind blows them

She's in motion as usual to the tune
It's a luxury to stay inside
I havent finished
singing outloud

Listen, gaggle gaggle
broo ah ha ha
thoughts unravel
run after her

The sun won the edge of the wind is cold two three
Nothing much but poetry
Ah ha I hear

INSTABILITY (WEATHER)

I would eat a lilac if it were a violet
Forcing the unstable air which is swirling around us
In the northeast to thunder & lightning
This air clears itself of clouds at night

We get the lilacs but have to abandon the rhubarb
To the new tenants, a few donkies & a goat
We get the first few mustard plants & some apple blossoms
We get the coldest air of the last frost, the birds
        arent even chirping properly

I must get back to the lilacs
So excited when I saw them first blooming in the back
        next to the apple tree
I nearly jumped for joy my heart beats rapidly
Because they are late & we are moving

Blossoms for Lewis & Charlotte who's here
The lilacs were so far away I didnt get to them
But I wont tell, I'll go with a scissor tomorrow
The scissor I'll hide in the woods tonight

For some strange reason I'll never say
I'll never have lived a more exciting day

JUNE DODGE

It's sixty two
& you can feel the balm in the air here
finally it's spring letters from outside
make me go cold yes the wind's still blowing
& from the north northwest of us we drove
all the way down River Road now you dont care
but the people living quietly with sense are there
& after reading Andrei's book
The Life & Times and so on
I think it takes longer than I thought it would take
& it's not so important to be literate
to change the season or the world
Families of other humans mate a sweet change
of sexes & what part of me still belongs
to myself is here isolate in sere

Harmony with elements I separate
from fear of harm the elements could do
to my family in winter's past
yet my devotion to a storm
is the storm's own fanciful knowledge

We dont go back to nature but we swear
the luxury of sympathy with the relationship
of the people to the land, it surprises me
to rest on something cold

SERIAL BIOGRAPHY

I was thinking what's the point of living life at all
I was very curt with the fishermen
I was reading "before she got really bad
        I used to take her to parties & things in London"
in Tom Raworth's *Serial Biography*
Death is always in books, you cant get around it,
        even if you never read
You just glance at things
Lewis was working in the room in the path of the
        threatening cracking tree
Of course you may trespass, I said
If the tree falls will the shelter of the house give
        protection or more danger
Live wires is a phrase I used to hear
I was going to a Puerto Rican dance in a churchyard
        in Brooklyn
no not a cemetery
The boys there they only dance the slow dances
Hold you really tight & press erections into you
These fishermen they make alot of noise, they giggle so
No I'm not afraid of them, it's Friday & people make some room
To drive up to the country
Where they fish & yell & maybe get erections
        which they then fill up with another person
        who is in their field of vision
Oh I dont feel cynical about erections but about death
        & all the diseases it causes
I'm full of it is a phrase I used to hear, it means
        you're full of shit
Bullshit, we watch the coaches mouth the word when they
        hear the call
Oh I guess poetry can be about all of this,
        what can it be about but those raucous fishermen
        with their brand new equipment, it's spring, saying
        can I trespass here

I said raucous when I meant to say stupid, the fishermen,
        filling my pen with grace
But what if the tree should fall on Lewis
I'm going to call Dave Tyler the tree warden now
And forgive us our trespasses
For the tree stands, he wasn't home, over the house,
        but for the forest, where they fall down with ease,
        over the river, over the trees, into an audience sitting
        in a patch of grass, I believe in ghosts when the door
        slams, it's my awareness of you
(I saw Mr. Tyler in the bright sun this morning & he said
        there was no real danger of the tree falling at all).

ABOU

I may babble about directions
& I may not spend much time on it
You can write it faster if you do
But when you dont, I am just saying
it's fine to have an audience
after having a family
with a fine smooth mothering wind blowing on it
to tell stories to
& somehow that was the gist of it
telling stories to madmen.

I used to tell stories to madmen
before I had a family
though now I'm running out of stories
& I repeat myself like a fine smooth mothering wind
blowing from the south southwest of us
so it's good to have an audience around
but when you dont, I'm just saying
You can spin a tale much faster
though you may not spend much time on it
stealing a moment, say, in the evening
to put into words what happened
ten years ago to the wheels of your car
whose engine was sound
on a 24-hour drive to Nova Scotia
you fall off a little in later years
when the demon hosting a dangerous poem appears
You become more simple & not to impose on the world
all your fears of starvation & danger, threatened
loss of love, an animal nature, a star even falling,
symptoms of revenge greed & even speculation, panic
at loss, the inevitable reprisal for the investment of
the whole being, fear of sickness & disease, bad habits
overtaking you, the whole constellation of the sins of
the fathers & mothers, & their investments, & their loss,
the problems of the planet & of the next fifty years,

even the danger inherent in passion . . . You desire to
control your own destiny, I wont speak of these things
at all, I wanted to say something new but I was
confounded with irony which I deny you, at least, when
the mind clears & I leave to your vision an innocent
field, which is blank, perhaps a spectrum is visible
on it, with a fine smooth mothering wind coming in
that direction.

CARLTON FISK IS MY IDEAL

He wears a beautiful necklace
next to the beautiful skin of his neck
unlike the Worthington butcher
Bradford T. Fisk (butchers always
have a crush on me), who cannot even order veal
except in whole legs of it.
Oh the legs of a catcher!
Catchers squat in a posture
that is of course inward denying orgasm
but Carlton Fisk, I could
model a whole attitude to spring
on him. And he is a leaper!
Like Walt Frazier or, better,
like the only white leaper,
I forget his name, in the ABA's
All-Star game half-time slam-dunk contest
this year. I think about Carlton Fisk in his
modest home in New Hampshire
all the time, I love the sound of his name
denying orgasm. Carlton & I
look out the window at spring's first
northeaster. He carries a big hero
across the porch of his home to me.
(He has no year-round Xmas tree
like Clifford Ray who handles the ball
like a banana). We eat & watch the storm
batter the buds balking on the trees
& cover the green of the grass
that my sister thinks is new grass.
It's last year's grass still!
And still there is no spring training
as I write this, March 16, 1976,
the year of the blizzard that sealed our love
up in a great mound of orgasmic earth.
The pitcher's mound is the lightning mound.
Pudge will see fastballs in the wind,

his mescaline arm extends to the field.
He wears his necklace.
He catches the ball in his teeth!
Balls fall with a neat thunk
in the upholstery of the leather glove he puts on
to caress me, as told to, in the off-season.
All of a sudden he leaps from the couch,
a real ball has come thru the window
& is heading for the penguins on his sweater,
one of whom has lost his balloon
which is floating up into the sky!

BERNADETTE MAYER, SUSAN SCHMITT & ANNE KUNZ

This is a poem I keep beginning & ending at different hours
        of the day & night
My mind's been drifting alot lately, maybe it's the weather
When we drive thru Hinsdale I think I'm in the Orchidia &
        I begin to tell you about Ridgewood
Or a story you've never heard before: when I was 11 or
        12 years old Susan Schmitt had a baby brother & his was the
        first penis I ever saw

Everybody was tense & on edge
The Cleveland Cavaliers were tense & they threw the ball away
I was on edge, it was during an electrical storm
Never use your vacuum cleaner!

An orange jeep drives down the road
It's been snowing all morning, May 19
I don't know what will become of the fruit trees
The fishermen have become greedy & rush eagerly from
        their cars
To catch more fish than they can carry
Do you think a poem must have something dark or consistent
        about it?
Clark & Susan are coming in the snow so you light a fire

It just won't get any warmer today, tornadoes in the
        poem factory
Or tournedos, boeuf, it's fifty degrees & I am ambling down
        Second Avenue in the hopes of finding you some furniture, I'm
        eating a teething biscuit & waiting for the Rheingold
        maiden, as the birds are chirruping, to return my call so
        that I can assure you of a permanent home
When I think of all the people who are really still alive, & I
        believe in them, then I know that we are & will be
Who knows? No matter how many fascists attack the baby in my
        dreams, that man was II Duce, I saw him, without a doubt
Writing this I want to fuck right now to ward off all the

fascist soldiers who were conspiring to make the little
priest, Edmund Brown, so late to meet the nun, it was past
their bedtimes
Fascists like Sheila Ward who married a doctor after becoming
a nurse, she was the captain of the varsity basketball
team, Susan Schmitt whose father poured milk from a cut
glass pitcher, Anne Kunz who lived on Catalpa Avenue
& married Linda Baumann's lover who had gone to military
school & Linda Baumann whose father's picture in an SS
uniform hung in her living room & whose mother told me
fucking gave you wrinkles, Mary Farrell who married a
lawyer from Rochester, her mother forbade me ever to darken
her doorstep again because I had given Mary a taste of
Scotch
Chivas Regal in fact
And Laura Cashdollar who was dark & made out with Freddie May,
Janice Laurino, who got pregnant by Michael Layton whose
real name was a long Polish word, & Mary Reiser who told me
that letting a boy press against you could get you pregnant
& Maria Heurich whose mother conducted sewing sessions to
make kimonos for the orphans of Taiwan
Oh Lord, forgive these battered Catholic women & thanks for
reading to me
From the Complete Works in my infancy

BARBARA WALTERS

I have no place to put the coats
If I did have a place to put the coats
That would mean I would have carried
My uncle's coat containers, whatever you call them
From Ridgewood to 11th St. to 9th St. to York Ave.
        to 26th St. to Great Barrington to Grand St.
        to 2nd Ave.
& then to here so I could
Put the coats in it to move them to Lenox
I remember Rosemary asking the Railway Express men
To take a trunk full of books
Down the stairs once
"What's in this trunk?" they yelled.
"It's full of books," she said.

"You're crazy," they yelled back.
This is what I think when I pack.

A ROUND OF BRIE

Da ya Da ya no mail
Cinque fois cinque foil
A man gets out of his car
I relinquish my hold on
My head, my bed.
Psyche, small igloo door.
Ah gah. Nadja
Small wonder door, if he
I feel small doors blow open
In to my face, baby stands up
I must be rushed, soft cigar box
holding the safe door closed.

Different voice a comment
On rushed or anxious calm town
        of many voices, a quiet descriptive
        place
So, secrets
Head looks down on secret thoughts
Embodied in cross-legged person
Abide, a time, be around
No counts against one
No stopping.

Babies are distractions
Time flies, you get away with it
Agreed disease
But in between one
No Civility, no age is modern.

We should go shopping for the igloo
Fat era, larger beer
Minnehaha
Like a long walk looking at
The learning to look at
Nature, oh Marie it wont be difficult

To be thee & not old Lord Byron
Who inherited land.

I write my writings at a price
River of Delectable Ice
Disease did you forget your keys
For her to be so much greater
Than myself would just be a chore
For her own good I would like her
To run in sentences, she will not.

Nothing more memory is tedious
Than an ingenious heterosexual.

INVASION OF THE BODY SNATCHERS

Moon out and no snow yet, November first
The first anniversary of our wedding and
The day before election day, 1976, yesterday
Was Halloween, next Friday I have an appointment
With the dentist and the following Tuesday is
Lewis's thirty-second birthday, exactly one week
After that Marie will be eleven months old.
The day before yesterday we turned the clocks back
One hour which made it seem like every day
Will have an extra hour in it, not only of darkness
But of just plain time, the time I used to spend
Skipping lunch is longer, the time for dinner
Is too early now, the time for sunset comes too soon
The time between dinner and Marie's bedtime is too long
When it's time to go to bed there's still a few hours left
To read, I'm dreaming twice as much as before
I spend all my new time lying in bed thinking.
Last night I saw "Invasion of the Body Snatchers"
And tonight when I came into my room to go to work
I found an old seed pod on the floor by my desk.
In the movie if you see one of these it's time to die.
It's time to write some letters, good cold air
Comes in my window, it wakes me up, we had a bottle
Of champagne and Marie went to sleep without crying
It's time to read *Fielding's Guide to European Travel*
And the *Alice Toklas Cookbook* again, a few books by
        John McPhee
Our new American Heritage anniversary dictionary,
The Adventures of a Mathematician by Stanislas Ulam
And *The Wild Boy of Aveyron* by a behaviorist psychologist
About a boy brought up by wolves

LEAVES FALL DOWN

On the fresh snow in town
It's a small storm
Beginning as rain
Hurry Grace

I watch it change quickly
To big misshapen flakes
Coming out of the sky
At us and it sticks

There's one thunder crack
The willow tree's yellow today
We have a visitor Grace on the way
Now the light is clear gray

The snowstorm becomes our livingroom
And lays its ideal light of snow
On Lewis's face at the window
Watching everything with me

The dim yellow light of fall
Makes white people look pale
Now we pick up our winter tan
A true complexion from the snow's spectrum

The color strikes me suddenly
We stand at the Worthington window
In memory in field on field of snow
Now it's getting dark in that quick way

Was this the storm from Indianapolis
That took away the pallor of that city
As reported in the news
Hurry Grace we can discuss it

MARIECHEN

I see that men, no, people need a proof
That men must have a proof and women will demand one
They do, like signs of athletic feats as examples
You pull all the Pound and Williams books down
Today some poets were sensible the best was Japanese
My own poetic failings are one sound and two image
Also I'm not kind and generous enough
Like Aert de Gelder I'm a maiden madwoman
I have no ideas about any objects to be told
But I hope to have one before you are two
Mathematicians and poets worry about their ages, years old
All day you look at me and I look at you
What will poetry do?
I don't know what we should do
Blue truck drives up the alley to the plumbers
I see men behind those dark windows
Having a festival or a feast
Carrying boxes of edible lobsters down from the upper floors
And lights flash on in the party room
As the upended truck out back forms
A judgment on my fantastic observation
Of stone-willed and cold,
New England's hedonistic wizardry

WHO WANTS TO GO OUT INTO THE BITTER WIND

for Lewis

I see the woman from Loeb's market
Running through every alley in town
She keeps close to the warm sides of houses
We do, we want to go out
No, Marie hasn't had two feet in the snow yet though
I see her running back now the way she came
Like a bird who must come out past a certain tree
If you are following its path by instinct
She looks like she's carrying a golden egg, a precious box

Then my view of the back porch and a child is lifted up
Where a night or evening light goes on behind red curtains
Something taken out to the yard, left out
The grand idea, don't ever worry about old age,
Please. As long as we can move from room to room
Or Paris to Rome, I don't care, the sexual assimilation
Of frescoes or the marks in caves like a good teacher
Or a woman who comes up against you, another woman
Limps down School Street in a bright kerchief

Though my heart is out on the roof of the red
Structure today in the conceived triangle for leaves
To cluster and I am a swimmer and a flyer in and over the town
A fat checkered man in a fedora
Carrying a box and a bag frequents this same red alley
I doubt another day could change another year
Age repents when I tell it an ambiguous idea

In your first year you already had a sister
Me too, you're only six months ahead of me
And our work done today we don't take a taxi
Home to an apartment in New York City

Baby decides that the 33rd year is walking
And talking, the second year to be married
As conceived by the pen any thought then
Is only two rooms away as when
You were born and in your first year
We have no sled, my pen
Terrifically conceals I love our adaptation
Of the dreamlike tree of the snow-roof
I made for you, never predicted
The ill repute of two
Studying man and maiden would be turning golden
So soon in the extremities of November's fine gifts

Two hands slowly say or see the quick woman again
Running back in the dark afternoon
That has gotten the feeling of an old day
And old confidence, yes I can do anything as
The piles of sand and gravel, the colorful hats are on for you
And the woman comes back for the fourth time today
In more than her 44th year with the mail
This time we all do all the same things
Over and over like the post office truck, parked again

And I see I can speak better of sight
Than an invention, fever calms the sky again
Coming to an end, a suspended act of snow
Like electricity not on yet, snow and evergreens
Line the yard I will build
With glacial sand and columbines which are blue

As if poetry supports the empty world
And isolation demands it but if people line up
In our sky, tacking up posters, they're doing our work for us
I always know if I see no person on the street
Or out my window who is not my own creation
Then I am a poet and my family of poets
You are the Father and I'm the Son
And Marie in all her powers
Breathing and inspiring new air

Through your lips above my determined chin
She then speaks as the ghost in the crib, holy

Snow and a trinity
All celebrated formally
On the anniversary
Of your history here

MISNAMED MY STUDY

This morning this cold morning
It's flurrying and the sky is green
In the west maybe from the radioactive cloud
On its way around the world
For the second time, I guess atomic bombs
Are better for a flat earth where clouds
Drop off the sides of it when done, anyway
On this morning I'm up at dawn though the sky is
Porcelain pink and green at the edges, I'm a worker
Having dropped off to sleep with my husband
Last evening like logs rolling over at nine p.m.
Because of the surprise of the warm bed
Full of blue and orange trucks, we each dream
Long dreams about going whole hog into winter.
It seems a little rudimentary like the tail of a pig
To wake up and go to work when you don't have to leave the room
Or get into a bus or truck to exchange news
With the other workers. I sit by an open window till the cold
Makes me feel I'm up in the eastern mountains
I observe. A big wind comes in lashing paper
Against pen and I wake up suddenly to see
That everyday I am expecting a visitor
But sort of hoping, nervously, he or she
Won't really come as if to preserve life exactly
As it might be or even is without the addition
Of any final perfection of the instincts
That might then suggest losing everything,
The third man or something, the checker.
I notice there are always two stories going on:
In one life everything's going wrong and it's cold
And though it's cold in the other one everyone
Carries boards just a few feet's distance to make a new pile
In a slightly different place, to get them out of the way
Or off the truck and the women stay inside their houses
Till late afternoon when they flood the markets
The second life is the sillier and less dramatic one
Another board goes down, making seventeen like bells
And morning's earliest business closes
Doors and windows to my poses

NO WILDERNESS LEFT

So step into your street shoes with the vanishing writers
I am a dim reflection of the pedestal of arches, Ionic columns
I became a connoisseur of airports or of television
I don't drink ink, we do an old-fashioned thing, writing our books
    and poems
When actually everybody is stepping into our shoes rapidly

Now, every one of Lenox, put down your autobiography!
I dare you, you do it, I wish I were Nancy, more for it
Or like the people of Japan who never get to know each other,
    never have a friend
I wait for my silly body to take signals but it's slow or else
    I'm much too fast
I watch television and imagine the whole life of each person I see
    because the t.v.'s too slow for me

As everyone watches I meditate as I see because at night I get too tense
Waiting to see if someone will notice that I've already danced, free
    form, in the morning
To keep my spirits high. Oh today I admit it I didn't dance
Being a religious person is like sealing up the hole in your head,
    don't you think?
A baby's delivered today, related to me, Lenox seems hostile

No wilderness left, I long to make a dreary cellar out of the glorious
    Ionic columns
I was going to hide from you all night and read Proust, no offense
Lying abed in Ray's scarf and Ray's good woolen sweater, and there
    aren't too many of those left
But thoughts of thought are drear as the cellar where
The same suspected flying squirrel who finds a roost in our house
    might be accidentally offed by the landlord

For a fight he had with a pigeon on the roof, perhaps because we dream
That the cops have come again to harass us, skidding all over the
    sidewalks

In an attempt to be human and actually they desert us and we go to a bar
But we can't wait for the beer because someone's ordered a bra
Or worse, these same police are only a dim reflection of my tough heart
  in the window in a scarf

I mean I am a barely photographable image in my own window
But I like to confront my self this way in Ray's scarf and Ray's
  own good woolen sweater, cast off and given
My wedding ring reflects the light as mothers unite if anyone can
I have Ray's boots on too and the pants I bought at Louisa's
And my own long underwear, a scarlet union suit

Could another woman in an equal set of clothes be so vicious and
  alarmed, we discussed it endlessly
As to turn fate on herself in the form of her own mother
Who must then relieve her of her own worst thoughts and fears
By mothering another newborn child, well, let's wait and see
Let's turn a step to Mabel Mercer, did you ever cross over to Sneedon's?

And who knows then what we must do to relax, afterwards
Let's dance around, getting dizzy
Knowing that healthy reactions are the origins of all fears
Of spinning and dancing and thank you too much for the flowers
Anyone feels it

When you spin around too much and stare into the eyes of the person
  spinning with you
You see the earth and house and all windows go past too fast
And then you die, I do, I die and I'm no dope, I came here for a reason
Did you ever cross over and I am not afraid of my own heart beating
Oh yes I am, the same with dancing, or of the blanket cover of snow
  now falling over

To get us into, like Buffalo, a big emergency
Thanks for the flowers, a baby's now born, whaddo I do! Yes, no,
  there's a life here
I tell this emergency the latest, my ideas one by one
As if they were the thoughts of a wild Antarctic returning
And the glacier melting on us, this is not my own debris

I accidentally miss you, the reader who says
That's a circumference bounding all my feelings
And for once I'm not the helpless writer, you're the helpless reader,
crossing over
Yet I'd written I sewed my soles back on my feet for a reason
They did come off! Frostbitten
As only two who went to the woods to work in one winter
Could be, or entertain the thought of going on forever. All past
and over, just that season

Now a sodden thaw, a bourgeois expectation in a house
That's a big baby, more Arctic and like a father in its entirety
Than here, almost, where only the human mind has power
Among these fifteen walls, who ever had four?

I am mentioning this snow that's falling now
I am marking it in my book: big snow, a baby's born
I admit it's still so light but it's been so cold
We rate a larger storm, a first-class Buffalo winter

I form myself on you, asking for more time
As if the winter roll of pictures, if I could ever finish it
Would be a way to show you and then I'll show you
All my environments clear as the man who waves to me

From his big American sportscar down in the alley
This man who might have known me as he saw me drop everything to become
The star of the dream I dreamed up here where
I lapsed in my own preoccupations to become the real owner
Of a big landscaping firm with two earth movers, a cherry-picker
For tree work, a machine to furrow the ground and sow seeds
And my own snowplow idling in the yard

You are not my first love but our intelligence as a people
Doesn't depend on eating or, percussion, your own mother in the soup
Children are up past the hour where
They couldn't torment you in the boat
That was fishing for night's daily dinner
The moon wasn't visible tonight and the stars aren't there

All things fall off my table as anger then hope makes room
For only your wild heart to be sublime

1977

New England is interesting
Suddenly all the snow is in Buffalo
And we've only got four feet so far
It was minus one this morning and two this afternoon
But the snow belt seems to have been loosened
And the mountains around us protect us
From the terrible lake effect and off-shore humidity
The Berkshire Gas Co. reported that our weekend
Conservation effort has been a success
But an evangelical organization called The Bible Speaks
Is trying to take over the town
Some buffalo got loose on East Street
And the Jiminy Peak ski lift fell down
A one-year-old child walked out of his house this morning
Wearing only his pajamas and some shoes in the freezing cold
But someone found him right away
And an old mansion Andrew Carnegie sold to the Jesuits
Is being turned into a medium-security prison
They may flood the wildlife sanctuary to make a new reservoir
Or else they'll have to pipe the water in from Lee
Where a boy set his house on fire to murder his grandfather
We had four armed robberies last year
And Lewis was arrested
For not paying a ticket he got on Hurlbut Street
For having no inspection sticker
Matches aren't free in Massachusetts
But you can get them at the bank
In the market all the chopped meat is packed for fifteen people
And if you go to the counter and say, "Could I have half of this?"
They throw the other half away
When all of the Florida oranges froze
But that is a whole other story
There are three town crazies who are actually shell-shocked
        veterans of World War II:
A man who mumbles into his cigarettes imitating different stars
And sucks chips to warm himself in the market lobby

A man who used to eat cream cheese on the steps of the Lemon Tree
I saw him today at the market buying cream cheese with chives
And a man who says he never took a bath
The ground is frozen and the prices of all the newspapers have gone up
After a storm they plow the car in
And we dig it out and move it around to the plowed part
We went to buy some whiskey but the liquor store was out of it
The shelves of the small local grocery have stuff that's so old
The prices are too low
The icicles in front of the post office reach down to the ground
And a couple who went in there got stuck
Because their car door froze shut
When the plowed piles of snow begin to get in the way
Two trucks come and take them to the snow dump which is the
        children's playground
Some animals are fighting on the roof all the time
And sometimes they seem to come down into the walls
The bookstore sent back most of its stock
And the library closes early to save fuel
Dee's department store is having its mid-winter sale
Harpo is walking his new little dog past the post office
And a giant bear-dog sitting in a hole in the snow
Tried to attack Marie in her stroller
A man left church the other Sunday
Shouting "It's beautiful out!"
The local optician's left town in a hurry
The local doctor eats fillet mignon and fresh asparagus every day
And the health food store is having a special on lox
The two banks are warm and the drugstore is hostile
The ideas of people in general are not heartily sexual
The lights went out and the town is opposed to the prison
Because they're afraid all the prisoners' relatives
Will want to move here, the selectmen announced.

VERY STRONG FEBRUARY

A man and a woman pretend to be white ice
Three men at the lavender door are closed in by the storm
With strong prejudice and money to buy the green pines
One weekend fisherman and blue painters watch
The vivid violet winds blow visibility from the mountain
Beyond the black valley. That means or then you know
You're in a big cloud of it, it's brilliant white mid-February
A week or two left on distracting black trees
Before the brownish buds obscure your view of the valley again.

Looking for company four dark men and a burnt sienna woman
Come in for three minutes, then bye-bye like a gold watch left on the chair
Or part of the sum of what big white families think up
To store for long yellow Sundays to eat for brown ecological company.
At some point later gorgeous red adventure stops, did you forget
To turn it down and laugh in the face of the fearful white storm anyway
Or picture it brilliant blue for a further Sunday memory
In a coloring book, you talk as lightly as you can
Refusing a big pink kiss, you burned the Sunday sauce
Of crushed red tomatoes, you turn it down to just an orange glow.
This particular storm, considering the pause and the greenish thaw
before it
Reminds me in its mildness of imitating a sea-green memory that is actually
In the future, I imitate an imagined golden trumpet sound
Or the brilliant purple words of a man or woman I haven't met yet
Or perhaps it's a grey-haired man I already know who said something
yesterday
To a mutual friend who will give me the whole story in black and white
tomorrow
Or the day after, just as the big orange plows for the local businesses
Go to work to push away the rest of the white snow that will fall tonight.

THE HEART OF THE HARE

Tomorrow's Monday maybe we'll do some laundry
Clean clothes for one night in New York
I've got to hardboil some eggs for lunch on Tuesday
Pack a compact bag and stay healthy
Lewis hurt his back hauling garbage
This quick trip can't stop me from getting back
To work Wednesday or Thursday, only three weeks then
Till we leave again for another two weeks of distraction

And then spring with all its fevers and slow days
Will come and I don't see why the weather doesn't seem brisk
And energetic then but it will not and I'll be prone
Or likely to succumb to what is newly warmed or unfrozen
In the air as if the space between me and other people that
Was generated in coldness for this part of a year past
Or became accustomed to the cold's distance now suppurates or matures
And we become closer in the freedom of the thaw and thereafter
And as everything is growing my conscience grows with pain
A little pain or weakening, an enervation and I am febrile
And I have to lie down or get under the blanket to sweat for a night

That's it, I have to sweat, if the temperature
Is 40 or 50 degrees, if the sun is getting hotter and if I cannot sweat
Something grows in me unnaturally or unnaturally energetically
Even feverishly sexually, this could never happen in February
Or is it that a tree needs pruning or a plant
To be replanted or an idea to be covered over completely
As in a hothouse to grow unnaturally fast
With sudden new sprouts and quick roots to indicate
Good care has been taken in the winter for a reason

So to prepare for this short season
I find I must be circumspect and stolid for a minute
To show a strong emotion or eat curry before I'm ready
Might take my sheltered winter heart by surprise
A heart still frozen solid and beating too slowly

To thaw when a thousand faces appear on the street or at the reading
Each one to be recognized, even touched out of a memory
Each one still enduring the shedding of the bulky coat and heavy hat
Or head of hair, each one thinking to flail arms about and beat the air
But forced by an old habit only to be sociable, to visit more
Or walk around, each one wanting to be rolling on the real ground exposed

It's last year's grass still and everything's in order
It's a medley but no one's really rolling around yet
I'm upright and so are you, I'm shaking your hand warmly
I haven't seen you since mid-winter or even before, it might be
        safe to kiss
Yet I'd hope I wouldn't suddenly collapse or cry
And then my heart is sharpened and can be faster, is thawed, and
        it's the last thaw
So it's safe to greet the rest of you
Already the people are becoming throngs
Or thronging the streets, certainly there's no ice left
The fever's past, I might be older before next winter
And before we meet in silence again
Broken as our hearts imagine that winter's long, spring sudden
        and warmth allowed

Finally, or in the end, I would like to say that a speech or a poem
        in the month of March is not better nor any more logical, innately
        orderly or sublime than a sudden embrace

EASY PUDDINGS

I think that I shall never see
Easy puddings in a tree
You say you must type everything
You can't read your words in hand writing
Mary says she has a double or a twin
And now a triplet
And she is a skinny energetic person too
I dream of Sarah Thorne sorting out the clothing
I dream the doctor of the Incas, my doctor
Is you or Matthew Christmas Tree, our bookseller
I see both of you clearly with your awesome dark beards
Full of animal crackers, I joke with you
About buying a bra, I measure myself
I have a 38-inch bust, as they used to say
But with nipples excited by the tape measure
It's only 36, I guess this is not a decorous poem
As Donne or Pope would have set it all up
Fourteen hundred to eighteen hundred A.D.
In the western world we've got
Where the work of women holds up half the sky

And yet the desire to write tonight
Is borne, dare I say it, like a seed
On the wind and so on, we were talking to your mother
And she told us every detail of your sister's
Country rental, the home of a doctor in Putnam County
It's never been rented before, in 22 years

I have my fears about women
Deeply felt in my desires to please them
I know many Margarets who are so stark
In their admiration of other efficient women
Susans who are close to the ground
Alices who please and clothe us tightly
And a Grace who likes to be free of clothing
Like all the Emmas and their freewheeling breasts

I do know some Marys who are somewhat tight-assed
And even a Leonora, a Theodora and a Florence
And a Beatrice in my memory of what I might be like
I do not know any Pearls or Violets outside of books
But I've heard alot about a Ruby who was a black housekeeper
To a psychoanalyst, opals my mother feared
Had brought her bad luck and emeralds I wore
As my female birthstone, emerald rings
Brought as gifts for Holy Communion or
First Holy Communion, along with checks
Enough to buy a garnet centered in diamonds
Here is your mother's diamond ring, it's set in gold
New gold, white gold, platinum is too cheap
She took it off to wash the dishes, or too dear
A thick gold wedding band, they say maybe stolen from the tomb

I don't know, I'd like to see these men or women
Who steal the bands from tombs more than
I'd like to see myself duplicated
In another woman human being, I am too safe
With my poet's senses and ideas, held too bereaved
Of the grief of the need to steal
A vivid platinum sacred scarf or needle
For my new baby or stereo
After all women hold up half the sky

Your mother says
My temperament prevents me
I don't like to be confined
I say to her the same way you hate confinement
I must keep active in my mind
So little babies learn to speak real fast
French Latin and Greek come out
Before I ever demand my milk and shoes
And then I go

I say to the herbal doctor
There is a vivid grief in me
I fear the things that are not real

Childbirth and insects, tetanus never scared me
More than the moment I saw a sign
Advertising "Red Snapper and Peas"
At four dollars in a restaurant window
Several years ago, don't worry doctor
I'll be a good western patient, stoic in labor
And breathing joyously in its fruits for us yet later
I may sting the child, who knows
Someday my wild imagination will tell me
That the street has turned the world upside down again
I'll lose my bearings and speak for logic without peace
I'll lose for a moment the superstitions that sustain me
I'll forget how I look and love only New Englanders
I'll assume their pale brown frown
My yellow eyes will assess
Only the feeble crops of the government in the fields
I'll say to my children, now sentient
But still less complex
This world is lost, I'll say to my husband
We must vanquish this world and seek the new
We must deal a swift death blow to the monster
Else this life is death to us

You see though I seem to fear nothing real
In almost every case I am able to hit the nail on the head
The children and the parents need lively interference
And nature, and nature however ill from lust
Will set our scene, I defend our states of consciousness
I hate our allies our own moods and I feel large
I sweetly see the bourgeoisie coming evenly
To defend our comforts, we are artists
We hold up the sky, we hold up the end of the sky
We hold up the next part of the discovered sky
We try to hold up in the sky, we defend the uncovered
Part of the sky, next to half of nothing
We brazenly will hold up the sky for you
We will make holes in the sky for you
We will eat holes in the sky for you and for each
Our sky is full of holes, half the sky

Has been held up for you, wait now
I will hold up the rest and rest for a minute
I think I know you
Prairie fire, you have not come to be
Intimidated or to be claimed
You are not a child growing
In an unknown mother whose heart and fears
And chemistry are foreign
I will isolate and contradict you for a moment
I'll hold back and not meet head on
The tedious difficulties and complications
Of the Latinate languages and the false Greek headstarts
Of the western peoples, 1400–1800
I'll give you a charm from a dream of remembering
Warm swallowing and calm weary moments
Movement away from dense cause and a purpose

Give me a moment and I'll remember moving
Struggle is not defeat, from the part that fears
We must not overdo it, we are indigenous
To the parts that fear what is spilled over
I am here but I might as well hear
Anything from here to the next recognition
Of my historical reality, for now, Solomon
Of the Bible or a cow giving milk
And serving as a lecture or an example
In Avicenna's memory in an ancient philosophy
Of thought, I lose the silver for a moment
Or the moment, the Monet, the water lilies
The famous money stored in cash or borrowed
That encircles the finger of my hand
That is western and germanic and dark
And married me to you who study mysticism
And want to hear all about it

We get to this point, don't we
Wanting to know yet knowing already
And then what is it that we are to say
It's taken me long enough and in a poor form

As if a poor farm or pure form
Either would be a better place
For this revealment
Of a practicable immigrant
Sought for his or her knowledge
Gotten, if you knew
From the collision of gnats, the dead souls
With pure bright nursery moths in pink and yellow colors
At the window and we say
We are all so exhausted and excited by this time
And this tie together and this constant motion
Yet a mere speck will make us move in two ways
And we can guarantee only this
Once by the river, we will move each time
And once again, each day
Inside the house.

MEDICINE MAN

To immobilize a pigeon you cover the bird
With a cloth the size of a pillow case
Pick it all up and throw it out the window
Setting the pigeon free
Tobacco came from the Mohawks today
In the same mail
With herbal prenatal medicines
Prescribed by our man in Harlemville
And something else happened
It was the man-who-smokes-down-into-the-ground
He sat tonight in the library yard
With his big head hanging over his smoking
And when he left we saw he'd made a heap
Of seventeen Marlboro cigarette butts
All burned out identically to the ends
In a big pile of ashes in the grass

THE MARBLE FAUN

Daytimes it's eating and food
It's not that I've got a wish to imitate
Nights working and books
Or be another
But as all men and women want to be like or unlike
A particular mother
The milk for yogurt cools down
I wish it would cool faster
So I can't avoid it either
I found a book for my sister about old and new lace
A testament to Savoy's Queen Margherita
Not Savoy Massachusetts but Savoia, Italy
The author a woman named Cora from Chicago, 1893
My mother never ate yogurt
And brought home the bread in a white waxed bag
I swear the milk takes hours to cool
No more B-ls now it's hotter than hell
Milk down to 159°, watch and sit still
There's always the crack in the world to excite me
It goes down to China and then to infinity
Yesterday I got a letter from a friend who's a whore
I don't mean a proletarian streetwalker
But a prostituter of meanings
Of fears about old money
Sickness and old age
Now the silly moon is rising again
That paper tiger, I knew her when
Luckily no letters at all today
Only a note of thanks and a little gas bill

Things to do with milk, ice cream
I heard the tourists coming in my dreams
I couldn't sleep, I saw a big bear
The biggest wind blew the blue curtain into the bed
It was hot as milk, has the milk now shrunk
We've left 22 men on Elephant Island
Slept only three hours in nine days

I am the leader, at least I can read
While the heat subsides:

This veil belonged to the Empress who paid no bills
"Her love of airiness and simplicity in the use
    of Indian mull, so resembling lace"
I appeal to the cool and lacy milk
"Designs in fine linenlawn not light enough
    to satisfy her fancy"
This queen has a very fat neck
"One is worked in roses, the other in flowers and leaves"
Her waist's pulled in, she's got a baby too
"When everything Egyptian was the fashion"
Now the milk's down and the wind's up
"This queen surrounded by her family"
Stirring the honey locust tree
"And decrees of fashion from which there was no appeal"
I do touch each in order as I think
Some part knowing what poetry could be
No one's ever taken this book from the library
Since 1893, I swear
Moon's make it above the trees, milk's become custardlike in the
    tank I hope, friends enjoy the wind like fried food, I forgot they'll
    be up soon, can this be exercise, is it dry or wet in the air, I won't
    turn the lights on but you do if you like, we're in the Antarctic
    now, your bright shirt against the white even more gorgeous than
    before, I don't feel it yet, I'm thinking about the order of these
    ideas, I forgot to think in the library, empty where I could yell for
    you if I needed to without disturbing a reader, carpets on floors,
    the big globe, books on the missing link, nothing on social security
    in this whole library, this is the missing idea, money, and my look in
    the library, between the daytime and night I'm getting older, a big
    guy like a hairsplitter or grasshopper has come now into my room,
    he's feeling his way upward with five legs and two antennae, a long
    tail like a fat neck in back, the tree's still moving, this moment still
    tentative, capitalism and materialism still here, a book about an old
    man, a young man still at the south pole, a loud noise signifying
    death to me, a paper out the window into the wind, he's gotten
    further up the wall, head first like me, now fallen down suddenly

on all five feet, I've got the five aces again and I don't know how to show them, a big gregarious grasshopper head, starting up the same wall over again, he has no way of perching or being secure, but five legs give you dignity, no, there are six!

I know now the problem was I had looked incorrectly, that chapter ends as pudding then, now why this wind, I forget the moment where I please and do everything right and be clear, he fell again and every time he falls he comes closer over here, there's a dual purpose in the dictionary, I get informed and divinely then where everything Egyptian is the fashion, old Egyptian and old Persian, old Persian milk is perishing, he's on my box of letters now, far-fetched and full and fucking, that's the moon and its monkey deriving more stores of adjectives, maybe you've found the best rest in old ideas, he can fly too, nothing much to that moment with the unused books in the empty room, so warm though, now a frenetic one's come to slow the tune, cooling down, I don't rest as much as I have a purpose when I'm in here, these guys don't, they're out of their element as one would say or buzz, some other man in town is writing his autobiography, he talks to a woman about it, I'll see my sister soon, right here, and now they're biting me, can I be nimble enough to skip over moments and feel enclosed in a kind of heat, heat before scalding, no damage done, where I'll rest in old ideas, save part of the old culture and still be a hero every minute, I consult myself and forgive it.

I fall too under the shower of water
Old and new but never another

BABY COME TODAY, OCTOBER 4TH

Ecstatic experiences with nature
This is an automatic furnace
Do not drop or roll
Do not handle with squeeze lift truck
Handle with care
This is a piece of quality assured
Home heating and cooling equipment
The Ohio Valley Container Corporation
Made its container to stand
A resistance bursting test
Of over 200 pounds per square inch
Not an inch a metaphor,
These words are on my window
There is no pane, the first frost comes
The second baby, we'll have to
Turn up the heat, eat nothing
And breathe through a rose
Emulating the butterfly's patterns
And the repetitive indifference of leaves
Turning pink, color of the rose, so flushed
Orange color, color of trees
Ecstatic mists train us, no feeling
No feeling, only moving beginning
The pane crashed, baby falls
Between loose pelvis onto the sheet
Watches leaves blow wind onto window
Ecstatic poets bend over, watch the thin doctor
He's in the light, this is a chore or task
Leaves blow the rose upside down up and down the street
Interior blowing toward muscles and thighs
Bending up and down, pictures of people
The butterfly replaces the hat
Every inch of the sheet is ironed
Practice matches a new sculpture of thought in ephemeral
stretching
The space is no bigger than needed

Air and water all around, pennies in water
I foresee a taste for display in blowing up and down
The crown describes only fantastic gems in air
No loose signs of what the teas will do for you
Fear a moment of taking longer than the warmth lasts
The visitors and the coaches then speak of their intention
For time to deny any atrophy or waste, even the giggles
Later longer than warmth not in inches
But in wrappings of leaves for warmth and evenness
The warm colors, the cold blue curtains between the sun and the moon
After pretension to be singly devoted to one's task is swayed to love
Then tne simple movement from inside to outside
Become astonishment, red yellow orange and eyes bright
Sophia Crystal foretells as I foresee absence of memory who
    sings eternally
Only to sing more and more

WHY AREN'T WE DRINKING RHEINGOLDS TONIGHT

for Alice Notley

The Crazy Horse is open!
It's a beautiful night, a big white snow,
Two little girls laughing, it's a little night
I just went down for bubbles and a pie
All the hard edges are becoming soft
There's excitement in the air
I'm drinking my last Rheingold beer
The Rheingold brewery in Parsippany
Is closing down

There used to be a brewery in Brooklyn
Around the corner from my house
Lots of kids' fathers worked there
And in the Rheingold Maiden Beauty Contest
Each year I voted for the girl with red hair

Actually the brewery's in Orange
And not Parsippany
And in New Bedford, Mass.
Where the beer leaves for Lenox

It comes to us in brown glass bottles
With a red white and gold label
And the words EXTRA DRY printed in black
In a horizontal ellipse
Below the ornate German lettering: Rheingold
And then in script: Lager Beer
Brewed with: water, barley malt, corn
And Imported and Domestic hops

It's the cheapest beer
We can get here
It's the New York beer
It's the Dodger fan's beer

It's the hoard of gold guarded
By the Rhine maidens,
Siegfried and the Nibelungs
It's Wagner's beer in the Nibelungenlied
And the Ring of the Nibelung
It's the beer of the Volsunga Saga
And now it is no more
We must drink Rolling Rock
From Latrobe, PA, which smells like skunk

Remember the cans, tall and white, 16 ounces
With the red lettering
Actually white on a red field
Clean-looking cans of beer
Ah, it's cold tonight
There is so little steeping
Boiling and fermenting going on
I am dismal and I have no beer

I IMAGINE THINGS

It's a fine time to think it
I've got other rhythms and rhyme, time to think it's made by you, made by me, what's the time I think it's a better time to sound it all out, I must have found it all out before, before I saw you, before I met you, I think this time I might know more than before, this is the first time I feel I know it at all or all of it, too many people call, I feel I'm not a good poet, I'm half a poet, I lose my poethood, I don't compose knowing enough, I don't go far enough away, I'm too close to myself, I don't lose myself enough, I must free the language more, I free it too much, and now it's lost, lost to you and others too, I wing it, I wonder about it, I indulge in it, I listen to every word, I sing and I wonder every time, am I doing it wrong, I swim and I flounder, I go and I wander, I see but I go under, and when I am simple it's too simple for you and when I am .... wait, now I see what others are doing, they're imposing a discipline and saying now I can't speak of myself anymore, I must describe the wall of bricks and the little limited visa I've here, I must describe that man and his dreary coat, no, not that, but an image become of him of his years and his industry, further and beyond the lights of colors to what we deserve as we hear it thoroughly through our ears, no even further, and with whom to share, the time to type quotes out and make a system of thought, wait, stop endless rivers running and the word "deserve" running through them tonight, what to make of it, what, I still think more, I still think I've blown it or I've made it, I've taken too many chances or I've not taken enough, is there damage, is there damage to be seen so much later or to be swerved at in an instant, to be avoided, to be learned about, books to be not only written but sent out, books to be deserved by everyone, are there children in such a cloud of half-knowing, such a primitive cloud of instinct and feeling only, no talking, are there children watching what goes on, feeling only the unexplainable intensity of the house in winter closed up with double windows, are they intimating a greater release, are they wondering or suffering, just what are they doing, are they thinking, what is it, what will I do, where will I enter my plea to be at the same time different and forgiven, who will listen to me, and am I whole or am I all in pieces, one to be riveted back to another, like the nervous doctor implied, how can I expect them to read all I've written, how can I ever continue to carry you, carry you, through every room, through every change in the light in the color, I see our images in the glass too, I see myself and I see you, you point that out to me and I am charmed, you point me back to my highly visual life,

life of peripheral visions, life of a good woodswoman, who will notice if I slip that in, who will care if that's a dream I had, you don't pay, the loud sirens may now awaken you and I will have to go and put you back in, sirens and cars honking and screaming as if they were women in a hot-blooded movie, again I take liberties with you because I think perhaps you don't even understand what I'm saying, who are you, are you my daughter or are you my whim, my own excuse for living, the person I read to, my actual mentor, the one who trusts and trims what I say.

There is a past each of us is given, no not given as if it's wrapped and then presented but given in exchange for a moment of silence in the present, as each moment of love is past as I fear so heartily the loss of it wishing it only to begin again as quickly as the fire becomes the vivid red you cannot see but only see in those bright tones that could be any other color, I love you then in bright red, a color become out of necessity a denial, my sheer impatience with the past has made me the genius of the tight palms, in the future I must open them and bring out the shared color that hits me when I dare to simplify and be brief in the heart that now, is looking at time, and stumbles horribly, you are looking too, we speak these words aloud, in the words that my mouth can form independently, I needlessly love you.

RIVER ICE

The winter's long
We're gonna move south
We're gonna move south someday
I see a look on your face that could be inherited
I see a look on my face despite my bright scarf
That I am only ten years old, dark eyes not to be
inherited
Our dreams at night are unwittingly simple, you
have been arrested again, I am in a flood
You are being tested by the lady in the library
I am being asked to buy my own arts and crafts
and the silver's too expensive
So I make false teeth of oranges like the nectarines
And mushrooms that are out of our range, they cost
more than meat
My sister's dancing freely, a friend of mine is weeping
My daughter looks like me and all of us are hoping
To escape to the second floor, the surprise dream-room
Where there will be air to breathe above the level
of mounting snow
And now the ice floes have covered the streets,
they're running rapidly
A child will have to be carried above them to be rescued

Someday we'll escape and know that our beauty was sublime
Beyond the time we recognized it, we'll know
We could have gotten away with it, I can't stand it
When someone writes you an angry letter, I will fight
if you aren't adored

My dictionary tells me to remember my energy
And forget my clout, my bout with fears or my
standing about
In imperfect sentences, longing to be praised or
taller for the first time
There is a violence in the book that even belies
the rhyme:

A field of floating ice at the surface of a sea,
A piece of such a field broken off and floating free

Would I be crazy if I thought
The ice in the river was beating me up
For wanting to taste oranges in March, for beginning
to resemble you
For losing and gaining in an adjectival winter
A superlative instinct for loss, it's in the ribbons
of my hair
I wear a blue shirt a bright scarf and a dark sweater
Your pants in the family, you move the boxes about
You know I secretly know how good or bad you're feeling
As I sweep over where the boxes were, delectable ice

Formidable family at the risk of being ordinary
We yearn toward you, the medieval presence of a youth's
persistent ideals in the walls
Not American, too old for that, not yet dreadful or
asleep though we might wish for that
In our fantasies, in this house, we only seek to please
our own eyes
Tastes and loves and hatreds chime back and forth between us
Speaking when spoken to, magic rises to the ceiling,
a mystic nodding, all forbidden, who's looking
Who knows, like a part of one's appearance, you would have
changed it then
Later our eyes demand it be the same, you could kiss me
and feel what I mean

Drifting and looking, perusing, it's the window or
the mirror
It's the free dream or the spirit to change and be
requesting,
Demanding a dream in the spiritual ice of the window
In the marvelous ice of the eye, your spirit's reflection
my marvel
My love the elegant turn your drifting takes when we
awaken
Demanding to know what each other has seen,
how shall I put it?

SIMPLICITIES ARE GLITTERING

If all goes well I think two pens are open
At the same time I might be dying and not know it
End the line in the exact wrong place
Though fear of dying is different from the whiskey
I found in the wrong place, there's a crash
Someone says come quickly, I watched myself
From a perch on the ceiling, I saw the open window
And fear of the diseases that Clark says wait around
Goes away. Yes I want to be transparent
As you are when you fly, Jim Brodey flew
In my dream of the magazine where poets die
I eat my cake and fear noises too, I hurry
To write a sudden poem not as day is going away
But as I'm only here in the dark
As night is in its middle and I have no time
For words, like sunset or dreary dawn. I see too much
I eat and drink and smoke without pretensions each
Note I make comes flying back on the tape recorder
Dense and unannounced, garbled and meerschaum
Like a pipe for smoking beer, I listen
And breathe rapidly when I'm out to wait
To see how suddenly a gift will alarm me
How wasteful and quick stubbornness is, how glad
I'll be when you lock the door and refuse to let me out

The red roof is shovelled
I speak but I hear, I move each body around
Like a piece of furniture, away from the noise
I am making, this must be a quiet house, house of
Experiments, quickly chosen, mercilessly followed
Eaten so rich, so full of cream and dreamlike merriment
The happiness of torture learned to form a wing
I fly out easily to meet what used to come in
No speech is filtered, garble it, effect, defect
I used to know you yesterday, I burned
I suddenly know you but we have no time
Today I know your speech but I have no rhyme

I speak to you as Shakespeare, monitoring feeling
I speak to you as Valery with emotion but about things
I speak to you as Proust, I can't be brief at all
I speak to you hurriedly battering
Or as Gertrude Stein just bantering
I love to speak to you as Mallarme in jewels
And of a piece, I speak as Larry McMurtry
In the vast spaces of someone else's words
And the ideas of the opposite sex, I speak aloud
As Williams and Pound about my tree and the queue
For the bus, I watch you waiting there with them
I speak to you most as John Bunyan a little mixed
With Sophocles, I know what I can see
This allegory is as of a woman alone, Sappho perhaps,
But it's faked and more like Virginia Woolf, not her
Real name, I speak to you in Hawthorne's clear Latinate
Sentences, so spun on my own head, so owned by me
I speak to you of my feelings as he dismisses me
For being so Catholic, for being so divine
For trying to be so Ashbery and Kerouac all at once
For trying to be missing nothing, to even be Ted Berrigan
And his Catholic Catullus at the same time
And in the end each time I speak
I look around religiously as Dante did and I am meek

BEST OF FEBRUARY

Heavy heads and hearts are ready, heavy
heady homes, eating ground chicken hearts, the beefy
readiness to be here every day

Heavy merchants vending pendants, I only
sing

Heavy elephants treading the ground, I try
to step lightly

Eagles and sassafras trees, dogs barking
at me: "No! I don't trust him!"

Even certainties, every day is lore and
memory, an idea even an elegy creeping like a squirrel
up on me because I have the food

Levelling memories of dancing as walking on
the streets the sidewalk crumbles from mind's weight
the floorboards squeak, heaviness of a trance, some
pretending

Mixing vulnerable liquids, why are you
waiting for me, why does the wind kick you back

Eating, eating heavily of the forms of
address, eating meat in restaurants, eating shepherd's
pie or worms or humble pie, eating weeping

Eating ambitious weeping, a delicate glass,
a friend, eating entrances and exits, the relief of
goodbyes, the snow thrown in derision at the screen
where I am to be seen working

Working lightly in space, a form I trust is
visible, seeking sun out, working off this heaving

hanging vision, working humbly and succinctly toward the shore

Watching there, the expected waiting and rushing at the end of our meeting to tie all up, to meet the rest, and friends met, to become new

Spending all this freely and something coming to need me, language flutters, bending and frightening, I thunder and lightning, I say what I see

Seeing, everything bettering me, me best at my task, entering to watch and then leaving, leaving I only come back again to

Hearts and minds I adore their clear fresh air, their stuffy certainties and learned foods, your memories mentioning me, my eyes like ice in this night's sky, I clean, I wing it, I ask for more, only to become you and to sleep as you

I would lose my grace and I would answer meaninglessly in the words of another: "Lie down and wait!"

Waiting for meaning to assume me to consume you and to presume to begin again, leaving traces, leaving to stay, starting to solve in blunt English

What began, it escapes me, what I lost, it's meaningless, on its own now, of one's own what is derelict and what is holy, wishes torn to shreds, an easy way to speak in the dark

Speaking solemnly all at once, speaking only, speaking only once, speaking easily each chance you give me, speaking ice as I close my heart, speaking peace as my heart eases, speaking of you

It's good to end but the better end you give
me, I live here too, I know ending won't actually starve
me, I hurry to eat with you

1978

New England is beautiful
When the white snow totalling
Over a hundred inches for the season
Blows from the north northeast of us
Before the spectrum halo of the post office light
Covering the sunken caves
And sparkling mud residences
Within the old snow's secret buildings
Mixed with pollution from the cars that continue
To pass, willy-nilly, as the man who tends
The library yard walks down Main Street
Exactly on schedule each day saying
"Good morning," as we say "Hello."
There is no sign of spring in the snow
As I write this, March 3rd
We haven't given baseball a thought
The grocery store has changed hands
From Butch who drives an Eldorado now
To the Cimini's, a couple who smoke incessantly
The liquor license sold to the Price Chopper
Joe will move the Record Outlet down the road
And Rita has quit the bookstore
In a long-standing disagreement with Matt
Ida and John's 99¢ lunches have gone bankrupt
And the chef at the Gateway Inn
Gives cooking classes in what he calls
The cuisine nouvelle, the tablecloths are flowered
A lady in the bank today said she had to pay
All her bills though others live off foodstamps
She followed us to the market where I saw
Her cart was filled with dime novels
From the rack, she had just retired
From 24 years at G.E. and I saw her face
Was filled with fear, chickens have been cheap
This year, on and off, Earl the butcher
And the owner of the store, fat in his knitted sweaters

And joking about Donald Duck orange juice
Has fallen in love with me as butchers do,
His two-year-old son
Won't stay in bed at night like Marie, he often says
"I don't know if I'm coming or going"
Mary the checker sees the sun rise every day
And the German woman who works the fruits and vegetables
Will give you the best bananas if you ask her
Sometimes I feel suspicion and envy from the people I see
Sometimes just the camaraderie
Of dealing with so much cold and snow
The owner of the Norwegian paper company
Who advocates corporal punishment in the schools
Has left his downstairs office to run a paper factory
And so the hairdressers are expanding into his space
The girl downstairs who has violent fights
And bakes the spinach pies peruses Marie with suspicious
eyes
She hears Marie's tantrums and thinks that we beat her
I'm afraid to eat her pies sold at the health food store
at 40¢ a slice
The streets are covered with ice, I think I've now
discovered
All the density and obtuseness
Of the minds of New Englanders
When a pregnant woman is stranded in labor in the snow
They'll rise to the occasion and get her out, when
a thought
Threatens to cross the clean white sheet-surfaces
Of their pale, lined and long-suffering faces
They'll swat it like a fly, the man in the post office says,
Listlessly, "I've come for Mr. Dread's mail, he just died."
People often ask to see the baby
And say she looks alert like a China doll
One night mysterious sonic booms rattled all our windows
Russ Samet's place was taken over by a chiropractor
A certain Dr. Tosk whose name in Norwegian means idiot
A woman called me about the playgroup
And said her husband told her not to come

Because I was probably a front for the Bible Speaks,
The born-again Christians who own half the town
And I would lure her and her baby in to be proselytized
A couple in New Lebanon are fighting for custody of
a ticket for the lottery
Really this winter has gone on too long
The librarian said even the black man had the sniffles
And the reverberations of our imaginations
Are shattering the new storm windows
In an attempt to fly out at spring and catch it,
Catch something before all our ideas are deflated and
mauled
By the tedious presentiments in the hearts of the
Lenox residents
That nothing can ever be changed, no love is vital
No arousal as final as the weather prediction,
No anxious commitment to poetry transforms the wilderness
Of frozen emotion to something that is warmly offering me
An environment in which to feel free to sing

TO MEMORIZE THE UNIVERSE

I do not breathe easily
While death is in this commotion of air
I know my devotion
To love without recourse is not fair

Marie's asleep, looking pretty, we can resemble everthing
    but we can't be mad or sad, we can only be monsters or
    be happy, I can't explain it but I might die if
The course from mirror to mirror went unrehearsed and bad
I close the book
And tell my mother to get lost, is she the one, invisibly lost
    within and still to be seen
This precious pen connects me to the visible world like a singer
I can't sing, I close the book again, I have no way to judge it
I have no form
I may have written all these words out of a need to be alluring
    like a siren
I am no one and I see nothing, I see no images, I hear no sounds
Israel has attacked Lebanon in a "senseless reprisal" with even
    less thought and fewer ideas, nothing today is appropriate
I indulge in senselessly missing people who have died that I don't
    love or even know
Because I love their friends, their acquaintances
As Lebanon is contiguous to Israel
The orange I see is to you quite green
As we used to wear orange to enrage the Irish senselessly on
    St. Patrick's Day
I know nothing now about politics, I knew nothing then
    of the universe
I've only been able to memorize its parts, like habits
I know what a situation may contain
Your father loves to use the word "vignettes" to describe a scene
He loves to impress us with words and spell and pronounce them
In an effort to contain an explosion, his possible sensible love
Is hidden behind his back in his hands, your mother's love
Is in not venturing, it is contained

By education and objects, a personal knowledge
Of the quality of what is offered
For sale and for free in the world, my mother's love
Was in protection from aspiring to do too much lest we be
    disappointed
My father's love in the tension
Of making a desk out of a piano
Too bad he was so rushed and died as he wished
So suddenly and young, I'm in a hurry too
As I do what they forbade
Love openly a Jewish man of the middle classes,
Bear his heathen children, have fantastic dreams, write poetry
    and die
But I am made of these two others
And as their flesh, I bring them with me to the borders
I have not lost my mother's humility which never served her
    in death
I have not lost my father's tenacity which endeared him
    to those he competed with
For him I still act like a boy, for her I'm God's servant
And as this soldier I live in a war
I ask if I will ever recover
I wish to resemble only my lover

EVE OF EASTER

Milton, who made his illiterate daughters
Read to him in five languages
Till they heard the news he would marry again
And said they would rather hear he was dead
Milton who turns even Paradise Lost
Into an autobiography, I have three
Babies tonight, all three are sleeping:
Rachel the great great great granddaughter
Of Herman Melville is asleep on the bed
Sophia and Marie are sleeping
Sophia namesake of the wives
Of Lewis Freedson the scholar and Nathaniel Hawthorne
Marie my mother's oldest name, these three girls
Resting in the dark, I made the lucent dark
I stole images from Milton to cure opacous gloom
To render the room an orb beneath this raucous
Moon of March, eclipsed only in daylight
Heavy breathing baby bodies
Daughters and descendants in the presence of
The great ones, Milton and Melville and Hawthorne,
 everyone is speaking
At once, I only looked at them all blended
Each half Semitic, of a race always at war
The rest of their inherited grace
From among Nordics, Germans and English,
 writers at peace
Rushing warring Jews into democracy when actually
Peace is at the window begging entrance
With the hordes in the midst of air
Too cold for this time of year,
Eve of Easter and the shocking resurrection idea
Some one baby stirs now, hungry for an egg
It's the Melville baby, going to make a fuss
The Melville one's sucking her fingers for solace
She makes a squealing noise
Hawthorne baby's still deeply asleep

The one like my mother's out like a light
The Melville one though the smallest wants the most
Because she doesn't really live here
Hawthorne will want to be nursed when she gets up
Melville sucked a bit and dozed back off
Now Hawthorne is moving around, she's the most hungry
Yet perhaps the most seduced by darkness in the room
I can hear Hawthorne, I know she's awake now
But will she stir, disturbing the placid sleep
Of Melville and insisting on waking us all
Meanwhile the rest of the people of Lenox
Drive up and down the street
Now Hawthorne wants to eat
They all see the light by which I write, Hawthorne sighs
The house is quiet, I hear Melville's toy
I've never changed the diaper of a boy
I think I'll go get Hawthorne and nurse her for the pleasure
Of cutting through darkness before her measured noise
Stimulates the boys, I'll cook a fish
Retain poise in the presence
Of heady descendants, stone-willed their fathers
Look at me and drink ink
I return a look to all the daughters and I wink
Eve of Easter, I've inherited this
Peaceful sleep of the children of men
Rachel, Sophia, Marie and again me
Bernadette, all heart I live, all head, all eye, all ear
I lost the prejudice of paradise
And wound up caring for the babies of these guys

SLOPPY LOVE

Rosemary come visit me!
Incomprehensible spring, break out!
Into a show of flowers, all the trees Milton lists
And all their fruits but the one I eat
Knowledge to make earth a heaven
I can't fathom what I'm dreaming
Reggie Jackson, this nun, this stupid cheesecake,
That silly lemon torte I saw like a dream untrue
A dollar a slice, smoke and bickering flame
Why this rich woman, who is the clothes merchant,
Why this parade, what's the significance
Of Lewis's desk in the middle of the street
I have a feeling that Arab
Is an old boyfriend of mine
I don't get it I'm at a loss
Hardly can spring be thought to bring
Such sloppy love, the home I am without
When I daydream lost in the window, love's babies within
To be born in pain in exchange for the offense
Of mere curiosity as Milton put it, he only got it
From the Bible and blind wit, his energy overtaking
Historic ideas as knowledge outwits eternal life
Whatever that is, these mere ends, I have letters
From friends, a woman who will visit me, one who won't
A man who lost his job, men who write about their poetry
One who writes about mine, a woman who loves dreams
A woman whose baby wakes up at dawn and screams
A man who gossips, a woman who kids
Will I ever have time to repair the typewriter?
Milton said the angels threw mountains at each other
And left a hole in heaven when they fell,
In my Milton book, taken from the library
Someone's put a big black mark around the part
Where Adam asks if angels fuck, I wonder,
I remember reading somewhere people use poetry
To wrap up things at the bakery, that's from

Cyrano de Bergerac, so the poet gets back
By letting other writers eat cake for free
I met a girl in the post office who said
She didn't have time to live in her house
And stars, Milton says, work all night
To make creation apter to receive
Perfection from the sun's more potent ray
Can anyone deride me
For trying to make sense of all this, suddenly
The angel Gabriel comes to tell me this mood
Is transient, my love will be surprised
A squirrel living so far away
Moves in the same tree every day anyway
Like loss, all this confusion stuns imagination
As hunger impeaches the greatest art
I'll forswear to write letters, to dream and speak for others
If you will come and see me and take my part

ESSAY

I guess it's too late to live on the farm
I guess it's too late to move to a farm
I guess it's too late to start farming
I guess it's too late to begin farming
I guess we'll never have a farm
I guess we're too old to do farming
I guess we couldn't afford to buy a farm anyway
I guess we're not suited to being farmers
I guess we'll never have a farm now
I guess farming is not in the cards now
I guess Lewis wouldn't make a good farmer
I guess I can't expect we'll ever have a farm now
I guess I have to give up all my dreams of being a farmer
I guess I'll never be a farmer now
We couldn't get a farm anyway though Allen Ginsberg got one late in life
Maybe someday I'll have a big garden
I guess farming is really out
Feeding the pigs and the chickens, walking between miles of rows of crops
I guess farming is just too difficult
We'll never have a farm
Too much work and still to be poets
Who are the farmer poets
Was there ever a poet who had a self-sufficient farm
Flannery O'Connor raised peacocks
And Wendell Berry has a farm
Faulkner may have farmed a little
And Robert Frost had farmland
And someone told me Samuel Beckett farmed
Very few poets are real farmers
If William Carlos Williams could be a doctor and Charlie Vermont too,
Why not a poet who was also a farmer
Of course there was Brook Farm
And Virgil raised bees
Perhaps some poets of the past were overseers of farmers
I guess poets tend to live more momentarily
Than life on a farm would allow

You could never leave the farm to give a reading
Or go to a lecture by Emerson in Concord
I don't want to be a farmer but my mother was right
I should never have tried to rise out of the proletariat
Unless I can convince myself as Satan argues with Eve
That we are among a proletariat of poets of all the classes
Each ill-paid and surviving on nothing
Or on as little as one needs to survive
Steadfast as any farmer and fixed as the stars
Tenants of a vision we rent out endlessly

HELL AT LAST, YAWNING, RECEIVED THEM WHOLE

John Milton's sentiments don't hasten spring
More worsen winter's heaviness still in April
The golden window of the neighbor's kitchen
Shadows uninspired by the blind balminess of fever,
Spring's source of wakening with a hand to the brow
Or at the dictionary page, turning to look inside

Louis Malle's made a new movie, Lewis will have
A new book, Shelley will have a baby, we'll go
To New York like isolated babies and it'll be ninety
Degrees, a prophecy, isn't a movie harmless enough,
Ought not a book to change the world, won't another baby
Grow slowly to be even more hungry than this settled state of order
Can provide for, as the rhythm of a poem beats faster
Than your own heart making you speed up to match
And become exhilarated, pendant world of April, all this silly
Latin and Greek, meters, meticulous enjambment, unessential night,
Spiritous revival amidst the absent ground, who'll win
The pennant this year?

Occasionally I look to see if the late-blooming locust tree
Has fallen, a dead weight, on my window, if barrelling thunder
Has ignited a space above the road, what would burn there,
Fantasy's exhaustion, the sons and daughters of Memory,
Only a vision, contagious rolling flame to begin an Easter fire,
Its liveliness to destroy the face of this homely town

Listen to what I say, it's your neck too

In his demoniac frenzy, Satan left the eastern shore
Cold heart of the childish businessman, impatient nature
Of the harried mother, moping melancholy of the misled government,
Moon-struck madness of the old, pining atrophy of children
Dire was the tossing, deep the groans

Then verdant spring resumed her electric bargain
Ousted Satan, Milton and Blake, Shakespeare came over
And brought a funny air here, Dante got pickled
And sang on the lake, a couple of virgins danced
There was fucking and more books and movies, more babies
Made the afternoons pass, angels and birds on full sail of wing
Flew nigh in the sun, soon the pennant was won
And a pocket of poets everlastingly disarmed
The garbage government of fierce corrupted language
All men and women were free to sleep and dream a reverie
Of complex constructions of the rolling seasons
Each man's heart an artless memory of studious visions
Moving with a slightly faster beat for a moment in time

PASSOVER PLEASURE

It's not matzoh ball soup
It's hot matzoh ball soup
and a glass of sacramental wine
make blood rush to my head
as I leave the seder table
to nurse the willful, intransigent
and unpredictably regressing baby
born in November's first isolating blizzard,
today demands love from strangers to her,
talkative blood relations.
I'm late for the brisket and pancakes,
the yearly picture of Harry in his hat
I miss a little pleasure
a dereliction I will be accountable for
to God (this momentary fasting interrupts
my heavenly work and is harmful to the community)
I drink more thick red wine
with a white grape juice chaser
laced with fierce concentration
on the contours of your mother's face
Ray and her sister Fanny
whose husband died when she was young
whose son fell in love with his cousin
whose daughter had five children
and then her husband had a vasectomy,
he runs a bagel factory in Pennsylvania
and owns two Cadillacs
but won't let his wife hire help
because he doesn't want a stranger …
Elijah's in the house.
Don't close that door.

SPRING HOUSE

Tuesdays we always have fish

Flounder if we've got foodstamps

Scrod cod if we don't, are you prepared?
I definitely feel you can't do both.

What else did I see?

The year's first lilacs, May's full moon,
I'm trying to remember now

Do water fountains have beards?

There is a space in spring for arrangements and
compartments even forms, there's always a space in change
for that, there is a space in death only coherent as beginning
and ending fall and as they fall winter never ended, spring
will not begin, we have the heat of summer, wordy and deferential,
interrupted for travel, the light not long enough for the
overbearing way as light falls words fall short of suiting
the subject

Hold my coat for me, would you?

That house on top of the hill always catches the
best light, I wonder who lives there maybe a family of
knowledge making so much noise it sounds like a public pool,
bird sanctuary, softball game with the chimes chiming in,
eight o'clock, knowledge's babies asleep, still light out,
the gold sun's gone, a softer dusk than ever fell does with
more grace on the late-blooming trees than on those fully
leaved and left to be studied, identically full-grown already

A little image or thought, squeaking or twittering
animals, an echoic easiness thrown in that could be the whole
of it, all I've got to say

In the beginning knowledge was a tantrum, now a spendthrift relative he or she only steals cupcakes or an occasional lost dollar from the funny way we keep things in order, knowing exactly where the lost things are

You almost lost it again

Now it's history, another way of washing clothes in the sink, you can use the same soap twice if you do the less dirty ones first

As poem is as a mother so instinct does it work, distracts from the legal order to leave the house in a metaphor's style among simile's kindly loans as neat as a pin like a seed to the wind

But there was something else, the matrix for the matrimony of

I've almost lost it again

Phone rings it could be anyone, what was I putting together?

You can't rest in ideas like an old secure neckerchief, it's good to wear one in the summer when ideas are so brief

Without the endurance of winter's darkness on their light

And what of making up things purely spun from fantasy as if the instinct to forget could ever have a line like I am a Marxist, I'm an anarchist, I'm crazy as a loon

The beetle and the worm crawled and wriggled on the bottom marble step in such contiguity they became famous to us, were offered mink coats and foreign cars

We looked for them again and could only find slugs at the base of the dead elm tree, you can't be in love with me any longer, I prefer my dinner at the time we have it now so later I can write and be lively without thought to food

Alot of time's passed since the plaid shirt you painted became so still, the moon and all has moved, earth revolving, sun sort of still but benefitting us differently, now we can use it to grow corn and tomatoes, zucchini and other squashes and fresh basil and close concentric onions and borage for the bees

What text will tell me how to so benefit my own ideas?

My waiting for love's order to know me sensibly, for incomprehensible prose to become poetry

For the neat desire of an opposite heart to push seasons together in the way they never suffer

But only offer a mesmerizing order to what is remembered, propriety

Not only that

And its variety

And how it's almost lost like the last block in a series of twelve that make six puzzles among them

But something else whatever it is and where I can find it, no code message or perfunctory obfuscation of the following order however human however a mixture

But a demon of chaos, surprise like a virus or a wheel to be engaged in moving and sameness as between inexorable sisters

The slowness and unpredictable biology of that

Combined with the skill to meet moon and sun

And all that has position like this word

Redolent of self and repeating

Always seeming to covet thought, always almost lost

Unless I can regain it, unless I can be ordinary,
unless I can forget everything, unless I know everything

Each order, it's a moment, speaks a clear word

If I am absent and silent, I can hear what is
almost heard

I know my heart is better counted on than redeemed
at every pulse

You are my feelings, seasons the word, order the light
and history the dark of the day

And what is almost lost is time to change us fast
enough

To get away with your love for another summer's
repetition, it was identity but it's not that since

And this shape allows us to lose and lose completely

It was the order of the family in the house that
catches light

And now history teaches but forget that

There's time to be turning to the noise, it's
only sound, only a moment left

There's always time, sometimes it seems we must
die right away, never a moment left unless always sometimes
never have made a false spring logic of our light

And then I know we are moving again, bodies move,
everything moves

Like the afternoon I met you too fast, late fall,
cold and dreary, the streets were lively

And at that moment you and I looked so alike as
night and day as they say

Photograph by Lewis Warsh

New Directions Paperbooks—a partial listing

Adonis, Songs of Mihyar the Damascene
César Aira, Ghosts
An Episode in the Life of a Landscape Painter
Ryunosuke Akutagawa, Kappa
Will Alexander, Refractive Africa
Osama Alomar, The Teeth of the Comb
Guillaume Apollinaire, Selected Writings
Jessica Au, Cold Enough for Snow
Paul Auster, The Red Notebook
Ingeborg Bachmann, Malina
Honoré de Balzac, Colonel Chabert
Djuna Barnes, Nightwood
Charles Baudelaire, The Flowers of Evil*
Bei Dao, City Gate, Open Up
Yevgenia Belorusets, Lucky Breaks
Rafael Bernal, His Name Was Death
Mei-Mei Berssenbrugge, Empathy
Max Blecher, Adventures in Immediate Irreality
Jorge Luis Borges, Labyrinths
Seven Nights
Coral Bracho, Firefly Under the Tongue*
Kamau Brathwaite, Ancestors
Anne Carson, Glass, Irony & God
Wrong Norma
Horacio Castellanos Moya, Senselessness
Camilo José Cela, Mazurka for Two Dead Men
Louis-Ferdinand Céline
Death on the Installment Plan
Journey to the End of the Night
Inger Christensen, alphabet
Julio Cortázar, Cronopios and Famas
Jonathan Creasy (ed.), Black Mountain Poems
Robert Creeley, If I Were Writing This
H.D., Selected Poems
Guy Davenport, 7 Greeks
Amparo Dávila, The Houseguest
Osamu Dazai, The Flowers of Buffoonery
No Longer Human
The Setting Sun
Anne de Marcken
It Lasts Forever and Then It's Over
Helen DeWitt, The Last Samurai
Some Trick
José Donoso, The Obscene Bird of Night
Robert Duncan, Selected Poems
Eça de Queirós, The Maias
Juan Emar, Yesterday
William Empson, 7 Types of Ambiguity
Mathias Énard, Compass
Shusaku Endo, Deep River
Jenny Erpenbeck, Go, Went, Gone
Kairos
Lawrence Ferlinghetti
A Coney Island of the Mind
Thalia Field, Personhood
F. Scott Fitzgerald, The Crack-Up
Rivka Galchen, Little Labors
Forrest Gander, Be With
Romain Gary, The Kites
Natalia Ginzburg, The Dry Heart
Henry Green, Concluding
Marlen Haushofer, The Wall
Victor Heringer, The Love of Singular Men
Felisberto Hernández, Piano Stories
Hermann Hesse, Siddhartha
Takashi Hiraide, The Guest Cat
Yoel Hoffmann, Moods
Susan Howe, My Emily Dickinson
Concordance
Bohumil Hrabal, I Served the King of England
Qurratulain Hyder, River of Fire
Sonallah Ibrahim, That Smell
Rachel Ingalls, Mrs. Caliban
Christopher Isherwood, The Berlin Stories
Fleur Jaeggy, Sweet Days of Discipline
Alfred Jarry, Ubu Roi
B.S. Johnson, House Mother Normal
James Joyce, Stephen Hero
Franz Kafka, Amerika: The Man Who Disappeared
Yasunari Kawabata, Dandelions
Mieko Kanai, Mild Vertigo
John Keene, Counternarratives
Kim Hyesoon, Autobiography of Death
Heinrich von Kleist, Michael Kohlhaas
Taeko Kono, Toddler-Hunting
László Krasznahorkai, Satantango
Seiobo There Below
Ágota Kristóf, The Illiterate
Eka Kurniawan, Beauty Is a Wound
Mme. de Lafayette, The Princess of Clèves
Lautréamont, Maldoror
Siegfried Lenz, The German Lesson
Alexander Lernet-Holenia, Count Luna

Denise Levertov, Selected Poems
Li Po, Selected Poems
Clarice Lispector, An Apprenticeship
The Hour of the Star
The Passion According to G.H.
Federico García Lorca, Selected Poems*
Nathaniel Mackey, Splay Anthem
Xavier de Maistre, Voyage Around My Room
Stéphane Mallarmé, Selected Poetry and Prose*
Javier Marías, Your Face Tomorrow (3 volumes)
Bernadette Mayer, Midwinter Day
Carson McCullers, The Member of the Wedding
Fernando Melchor, Hurricane Season
Paradais
Thomas Merton, New Seeds of Contemplation
The Way of Chuang Tzu
Henri Michaux, A Barbarian in Asia
Henry Miller, The Colossus of Maroussi
Big Sur & the Oranges of Hieronymus Bosch
Yukio Mishima, Confessions of a Mask
Death in Midsummer
Eugenio Montale, Selected Poems*
Vladimir Nabokov, Laughter in the Dark
Pablo Neruda, The Captain's Verses*
Love Poems*
Charles Olson, Selected Writings
George Oppen, New Collected Poems
Wilfred Owen, Collected Poems
Hiroko Oyamada, The Hole
José Emilio Pacheco, Battles in the Desert
Michael Palmer, Little Elegies for Sister Satan
Nicanor Parra, Antipoems*
Boris Pasternak, Safe Conduct
Octavio Paz, Poems of Octavio Paz
Victor Pelevin, Omon Ra
Fernando Pessoa
The Complete Works of Alberto Caeiro
Alejandra Pizarnik
Extracting the Stone of Madness
Robert Plunket, My Search for Warren Harding
Ezra Pound, The Cantos
New Selected Poems and Translations
Qian Zhongshu, Fortress Besieged
Raymond Queneau, Exercises in Style
Olga Ravn, The Employees
Herbert Read, The Green Child
Kenneth Rexroth, Selected Poems
Keith Ridgway, A Shock
Rainer Maria Rilke
Poems from the Book of Hours
Arthur Rimbaud, Illuminations*
A Season in Hell and The Drunken Boat*
Evelio Rosero, The Armies
Fran Ross, Oreo
Joseph Roth, The Emperor's Tomb
Raymond Roussel, Locus Solus
Ihara Saikaku, The Life of an Amorous Woman
Nathalie Sarraute, Tropisms
Jean-Paul Sartre, Nausea
Kathryn Scanlan, Kick the Latch
Delmore Schwartz
In Dreams Begin Responsibilities
W.G. Sebald, The Emigrants
The Rings of Saturn
Anne Serre, The Governesses
Patti Smith, Woolgathering
Stevie Smith, Best Poems
Novel on Yellow Paper
Gary Snyder, Turtle Island
Muriel Spark, The Driver's Seat
The Public Image
Maria Stepanova, In Memory of Memory
Wislawa Szymborska, How to Start Writing
Antonio Tabucchi, Pereira Maintains
Junichiro Tanizaki, The Maids
Yoko Tawada, The Emissary
Scattered All over the Earth
Dylan Thomas, A Child's Christmas in Wales
Collected Poems
Thuan, Chinatown
Rosemary Tonks, The Bloater
Tomas Tranströmer, The Great Enigma
Leonid Tsypkin, Summer in Baden-Baden
Tu Fu, Selected Poems
Elio Vittorini, Conversations in Sicily
Rosmarie Waldrop, The Nick of Time
Robert Walser, The Tanners
Eliot Weinberger, An Elemental Thing
Nineteen Ways of Looking at Wang Wei
Nathanael West, The Day of the Locust
Miss Lonelyhearts
Tennessee Williams, The Glass Menagerie
A Streetcar Named Desire
William Carlos Williams, Selected Poems
Alexis Wright, Praiseworthy
Louis Zukofsky, "A"

*BILINGUAL EDITION